JA

GW00674918

1. **Sat. MARY, MOTHER OF GOD**
   ALL 479, Te Deum; DP Ps 119
   EP I (of Epiphany) 546; NP 11
   Hymns for Christmas Season

2. **Sun. EPIPHANY (Sol)**
   ALL 551, Te Deum; NP 1172
   Hymns after Epiphany from the Feast, or from Christmas Season,
   p. 385 and following.

3. Mon. Monday after Epiphany or Most Holy Name of Jesus (New)
   No official texts yet exist in English.
   ALL 816, Ant, Rd, etc. 575; NP 1175

4. Tue. St. Elizabeth Ann Seton (Mem) (1689)
   From Com of Rel 1554
   OOR 1554, Ps 834, Rd 584 & 1689, Pr 1691
   MP 1558, Ps 839, Pr 1691; DP 844, Ant, Rd, etc. 589
   EP 1560, Ps 847, Pr 1691; NP 1178

5. Wed. St. John Neumann, B (Mem) (1692)
   From Com of Pas 1428
   OOR 1428, Ps 852, Rd 592 & 1692, Pr 1695
   MP 1443, Ps 857, Pr 1695; DP 862 Ant, Rd, etc. 598
   EP 1449, Ps 867, Pr 1695; NP 1180

6. Thu. Thursday after Epiphany
   ALL 872, Ant, Rd, etc. 601; NP 1183

OR: St. André Bessette, Rel **(New)** (5)
   From Com of HM 1500 or Rel 1554
   OOR 1500 or 1554, Ps 873, Rd 601 & 1556, Pr (6) or 1559
   MP from Com, Ps 877, Pr (6) 1559; DP 881, Ant, etc. 606
   EP from Com, Ps 886, Pr (6) or 1559; NP 1183

7. Fri. Friday after Epiphany
   ALL 890, Ant, Rd, etc. 609; NP 1185

OR: St. Raymond of Pennyafort, P (1288)
   From Com of Pas 1428
   OOR 1428, Ps 891, Rd 609 & 1288, Pr 1290

MP 1443, Ps 894, Pr 1290; DP 898, Ant, Rd, etc. 615
EP 1449, Ps 902, Pr 1290; NP 1185

8. Sat. Saturday after Epiphany
   ALL 906, Ant, Rd, etc. 618
   EP I (of Baptism) 625; NP 1169

9. **Sun. BAPTISM OF THE LORD (F)**
   ALL 628, Te Deum; DP Ps 934; NP 1172

BEGIN VOLUME III

10. Mon. Monday of the 1st Week in Ordinary Time
    ALL 702, Rd 53 & Pr 56; NP 1275

11. Tue. Tuesday of the 1st Week in Ordinary Time
    ALL 722, Rd 57 & Pr 60; NP 1278

12. Wed. Wednesday of the 1st Week in Ordinary Time
    ALL 744, Rd 60 & Pr 64; NP 1280

13. Thu. Thursday of the 1st Week in Ordinary Time
    ALL 765, Rd 65 & Pr 69; NP 1283

OR: St. Hilary, B & D (1301)
    From Com of Pas 1734 or D 1763
    OOR 765, Rd 65 & 1301, Pr 1303
    MP from Com, Ps 769, Pr 1303; DP 774
    EP from Com, Ps 780, Pr 1303; NP 1283

14. Fri. Friday of the 1st Week in Ordinary Time
    ALL 786, Rd 69 & Pr 73; NP 1285

15. Sat. Saturday of the 1st Week in Ordinary Time
    ALL 807, Rd 73 & Pr 77; EP see below

OR: BVM on Saturday - 1642 & 807
    Rd 73 & 1642f, Pr 1653f; DP 816
    EP I (of Sunday) 821, Ant & Pr 78; NP 1269

16. **Sun. SECOND SUNDAY IN ORDINARY TIME**
    ALL 826, Rd, Te Deum, Ant & Pr 78; NP 1272

17. Mon. St. Anthony, Ab (Mem) (1303)
    From Com of Rel 1858
    OOR 848, Rd 82 & 1304, Pr 1305
    MP 1862, Ps 853, Pr 1305; DP 858
    EP 1864, Ps 864, Pr 1305; NP 1275

18. Tue. Tuesday of the 2nd Week in Ordinary Time
ALL 869, Rd 86 & Pr 89; NP 1278

19. Wed. Wednesday of the 2nd Week in Ordinary Time
ALL 891, Rd 90 & Pr 93; NP 1280

20. Thu. Thursday of the 2nd Week in Ordinary Time
ALL 916, Rd 94 & Pr 98; NP 1283

OR: St. Fabian, Po & M (1306)
From Com of M 1707 or Pas 1734
OOR 916, Rd 94 & 1306; Pr 1308
MP from Com, Ps 920; Pr 1308; DP 926
EP from Com, Ps 932, Pr 1308; NP 1283

OR: St. Sebastian, M (1308)
From Com of M 1707
OOR 916, Rd 94 & 1308, Pr 1310
MP 1715, Ps 920, Pr 1310; DP 926
EP 1721, Ps 932, Pr 1310; NP 1283

21. Fri. St. Agnes, V & M (Mem) (1310)
From Com of M 1707 or V 1777
OOR 937, Rd 98 & 1310, Pr 1313
MP 1312, Ps 688, Intercessions from Com; DP 946
EP 1314, Ps 1722, Intercessions from Com; NP 1285

22. Sat. Day of Prayer for the Legal Protection of Unborn Children
ALL 958, Rd 103 & Pr 107; EP I (of Sunday) 973, Ant & Pr 108; NP 1269

23. **Sun. THIRD SUNDAY IN ORDINARY TIME**
ALL 978, Rd, Te Deum, Ant & Pr 108; NP 1272

24. Mon. St. Francis de Sales, B & D (Mem) (1317)
From Com of Pas 1734 or D 1763
OOR 998, Rd 113 & 1317, Pr 1319
MP from Com, Ps 1002, Pr 1319; DP 1007
EP from Com, Ps 1012, Pr 1319; NP 1275

25. Tue. CONVERSION OF ST. PAUL, AP (F) (1320)
From Com of AP 1659 and Proper, Te Deum
DP 1029, Ant, Rd, etc. 1326, Pr 1325; NP 1278

26. Wed. Sts. Timothy and Titus, Bb (Mem) (1329)
From Com of Pas 1734
OOR 1039, Rd 122 & 1329, Pr 1331
MP 1749, Ps 1045, Ant & Pr 1331; DP 1050
EP 1755, Ps 1056, Ant 1332, Pr 1331; NP 1280

27.   Thu. Thursday of the 3rd Week in Ordinary Time
      ALL 1061, Rd 127 & Pr 131; NP 1283

OR: St. Angela Merici, V (1332)
      From Com of V 1777 or Tea 1871
      OOR 1061, Rd 127 & 1332, Pr 1334
      MP from Com, Ps 1066, Pr 1334; DP 1071
      EP from Com, Ps 1077, Pr 1334; NP 1283

28.   Fri. St. Thomas Aquinas, P & D (Mem) (1334)
      From Com of D 1763
      OOR 1082, Rd 131 & 1335, Pr 1337
      MP 1768, Ps 1087, Ant 1336 & Pr 1337; DP 1092
      EP 1770, Ps 1098, Ant & Pr 1337; NP 1285

29.   Sat. Saturday of the 3rd Week in Ordinary Time
      ALL 1103, Rd 135 & Pr 139; EP see below

OR: BVM on Saturday - 1642 & 1103
      Rd 135 & 1642f, Pr 1653f; DP 1112
      EP I (of Sunday) 1117, Ant & Pr 140; NP 1269

30.   Sun. **FOURTH SUNDAY IN ORDINARY TIME**
      ALL 1122, Rd, Te Deum, Ant & Pr 140; NP 1272

31.   Mon. St. John Bosco, P (Mem) (1337)
      From Com of Pas 1734 or Tea 1871
      OOR 1143, Rd 145 & 1337, Pr 1339
      MP from Com, Ps 1148, Pr 1339; DP 1154
      EP from Com, Ps 1160, Pr 1339; NP 1275

FEBRUARY

1.   Tue. Tuesday of the 4th Week in Ordinary Time
      ALL 1165, Rd 149 & Pr 152; NP 1278

2.   Wed. PRESENTATION OF THE LORD (F)
      ALL 1344, Te Deum; DP Ps 1198; EP 1355; NP 1280

3.   Thu. Thursday of the 4th Week in Ordinary Time
      ALL 1210, Rd 156 & Pr 159; NP 1283

OR: St. Blase, B & M (1360)
      From Com of M 1707 or Pas 1734
      OOR 1210, Rd 156 & 1360, Pr 1362
      MP from Com, Ps 1214, Pr 1362; DP 1219
      EP from Com, Ps 1225, Pr 1362; NP 1283

OR: St. Ansgar, B (1362)
From Com of Pas 1734
OOR 1210, Rd 156 & 1362, Pr 1364
MP 1749, Ps 1214, Pr 1364; DP 1219
EP 1755, Ps 1225, Pr 1364; NP 1283

4. Fri. Friday of the 4th Week in Ordinary Time
ALL 1230, Rd 160 & Pr 163; NP 1285

5. Sat. St. Agatha, V & M (Mem) (1364)
From Com of M 1707 or V 1777
OOR 1250, Rd 164 & 1365, Pr 1366
MP from Com, Ps 1254, Ant & Pr 1366; DP 1259
EP I (of Sunday) 677, Ant & Pr 168; NP 1269

6. **Sun. FIFTH SUNDAY IN ORDINARY TIME**
ALL 682, Rd, Te Deum, Ant & Pr 168; NP 1272

7. Mon. Monday of the 5th Week in Ordinary Time
ALL 702, Rd 172 & Pr 176; NP 1275

8. Tue. Tuesday of the 5th Week in Ordinary Time
ALL 722, Rd 176 & Pr 180; NP 1278

OR: St. Jerome Emiliani (1369)
From Com of Tea 1871
OOR 722, Rd 176 & 1370, Pr 1372
MP 1873, Ps 728, Pr 1372; DP 733
EP 1874, Ps 739, Pr 1372; NP 1278

OR: St. Josephine Bakhita, V *(New)*
From Com of V, 1777
OOR 722, Rd 176 & 1782, Pr 1789
MP 1786, Ps 728, Pr 1789; DP 733
EP 1791, Ps 739, Pr 1797; NP 1278

9. Wed. Wednesday of the 5th Week in Ordinary Time
ALL 744, Rd 181 & Pr 185; NP 1280

10. Thu. St. Scholastica, V (Mem) (1372)
From Com of V 1777
OOR 765, Rd 185 & 1372, Pr 1374
MP 1786, Ps 769, Ant & Pr 1374; DP 774
EP 1791, Ps 780, Pr 1374; NP 1283

11. Fri. Friday of the 5th Week in Ordinary Time
ALL 786, Rd 189 & Pr 193; NP 1285

OR: Our Lady of Lourdes (1374)
From Com of BVM 1614
OOR 786, Rd 189 & 1375, Pr 1377
MP 1626, Ps 790, Ant & Pr 1377; DP 796
EP 1634, Pr 802, Ant & Pr 1377; NP 1285

12. Sat. Saturday of the 5th Week in Ordinary Time
ALL 807, Rd 193 & Pr 196; EP see below

OR: BVM on Saturday - 1642 & 807
Rd 193 & 1642f, Pr 1653f; DP 816
EP I (of Sunday) 821, Ant & Pr 197; NP 1269

13. **Sun. SIXTH SUNDAY IN ORDINARY TIME**
ALL 826, Rd, Te Deum, Ant & Pr 197; NP 1272

14. Mon. Sts. Cyril, Monk, and Methodius, B (Mem) (1377)
From Com of Pas 1734
OOR 847, Rd 201 & 1378, Pr 1380
MP 1749, Ps 853, Ant 1379 & Pr 1380; DP 858
EP 1755, Ps 864, Ant & Pr 1380; NP 1275

15. Tue. Tuesday of the 6th Week in Ordinary Time
ALL 869, Rd 205 & Pr 209; NP 1278

16. Wed. Wednesday of the 6th Week in Ordinary Time
ALL 891, Rd 209 & Pr 213; NP 1280

17. Thu. Thursday of the 6th Week in Ordinary Time
ALL 916, Rd 213 & Pr 217; NP 1283

OR: Seven Founders of the Order of Servites (1380)
From Com of Rel 1858
OOR 916, Rd 213 & 1380, Pr 1383
MP 1862, Ps 920, Ant 1382 & Pr 1383; DP 926
EP 1864, Ps 932, Pr 1383; NP 1283

18. Fri. Friday of the 6th Week in Ordinary Time
ALL 937, Rd 218 & Pr 221; NP 1285

19. Sat. Saturday of the 6th Week in Ordinary Time
ALL 958, Rd 222 & Pr 225; EP see below

OR: BVM on Saturday - 1642 & 958
Rd 222 & 1642f, Pr 1653f; DP 968
EP I (of Sunday) 973, Ant & Pr 227; NP 1269

20. **Sun. SEVENTH SUNDAY IN ORDINARY TIME**
ALL 978, Rd, Te Deum, Ant & Pr 227; NP 1272

21. Mon. Monday of the 7th Week in Ordinary Time
ALL 998, Rd 232 & Pr 235; NP 1275

OR: St. Peter Damian, B & D (1383)
From Com of Pas 1734 or D 1763
OOR 998, Rd 232 & 1383, Pr 1385
MP from Com, Ps 1002, Pr 1385; DP 1007
EP from Com, Ps 1012, Pr 1385; NP 1275

22. Tue. CHAIR OF ST. PETER, AP (F) (1386)
From Com of Ap 1659 and Proper, Te Deum
DP 1029, Rd, etc. 1392, Pr 1392; NP 1278

23. Wed. St. Polycarp, B & M (Mem) (1395)
From Com of M 1707 or Pas 1734
OOR 1039, Rd 240 & 1396, Pr 1398
MP from Com, Ps 1045, Ant & Pr 1398; DP 1050
EP from Com, Ps 1056, Ant & Pr 1398; NP 1280

24. Thu. Thursday of the 7th Week in Ordinary Time
ALL 1061, Rd 244 & Pr 248; NP 1283

25. Fri. Friday of the 7th Week in Ordinary Time
ALL 1082, Rd 248 & Pr 252; NP 1285

26. Sat. Saturday of the 7th Week in Ordinary Time
ALL 1103, Rd 253 & Pr 257; EP see below

OR: BVM on Saturday - 1642 & 1103
Rd 253 & 1642f, Pr 1653f; DP 1112
EP I (of Sunday) 1117, Ant & Pr 258; NP 1269

27. **Sun. EIGHTH SUNDAY IN ORDINARY TIME**
ALL 1122, Rd, Te Deum, Ant & Pr 258; NP 1272

28. Mon. Monday of the 8th Week in Ordinary Time
ALL 1143, Rd 263 & Pr 266; NP 1275

MARCH

1. Tue. Tuesday of the 8th Week in Ordinary Time
ALL 1165, Rd 266 & Pr 270; NP 1278

BEGIN VOLUME II

Hymns for Lenten Season before Holy Week: 33-47

2. Wed. Ash Wednesday
ALL 49, Ps 1551; NP 1638, Hymn 38

3. Thu. Thursday after Ash Wednesday
OOR 58, Ps 1571 (May add Rd & Pr of St. Katharine Drexel, V **[New]**,
   Rd 2110, Pr [7] or 2118)
MP 62, Ps 1574 (May add Ant & Pr [7] of St. Katharine 2117)
DP 63, Ps 1579
EP 64, Ps 1583 (May add Ant & Pr [7] of St. Katharine 2125)
NP 1642

4. Fri. Friday after Ash Wednesday
OOR 66, Ps 1588 (May add Rd & Pr of St. Casimir 1698-1700)
MP 70, Ps 1593 (May add Ant & Pr of St. Casimir 1700)
DP 72, Ps 1598
EP 73, Ps 1601 (May add Ant & Pr of St. Casimir 1700); NP 1644

5. Sat. Saturday after Ash Wednesday
ALL 75, Ps 1607; EP I (of Sunday) 82, Ps 1076; NP 1625

6. **Sun. FIRST SUNDAY OF LENT**
ALL 84, Ps 1082; NP 1628, Hymn 38

7. Mon. Monday of the 1st Week of Lent
OOR 94, Ps 1102 (May add Rd & Pr of Sts. Perpetua and Felicity, Mm
   1700-1703)
MP 98, Ps 1107 (May add Ant & Pr of Sts. Perpetua and Felicity 1703)
DP 99, Ps 1111
EP 100, Ps 1115 (May add Ant & Pr of Sts. Perpetua and Felicity 1703)
NP 1632

8. Tue. Tuesday of the 1st Week of Lent
OOR 102, Ps 1121 (May add Rd & Pr of St. John of God, Rel 1704-1706)
MP 106, Ps 1126 (May add Ant & Pr of St. John of God 1706)
DP 108, Ps 1131
EP 109, Ps 1135 (May add Ant & Pr of St. John 1706); NP 1635

9. Wed. Wednesday of the 1st Week of Lent
OOR 111, Ps 1141 (May add Rd & Pr of St. Frances of Rome, Rel 1707-
   1709)
MP 115, Ps 1146 (May add Ant & Pr of St. Frances 1709)
DP 117, Ps 1150
EP 118, Ps 1153 (May add Ant 1710 & Pr of St. Frances 1709)
NP 1638

10. Thu. Thursday of the 1st Week of Lent
ALL 120, Ps 1158; NP 1642

11. Fri. Friday of the 1st Week of Lent
    ALL 129, Ps 1176; NP 1644

12. Sat. Saturday of the 1st Week of Lent
    ALL 137, Ps 1194
    EP I (of Sunday) 145, Ps 1208; NP 1625

13. **Sun. SECOND SUNDAY OF LENT**
    ALL 147, Ps 1214; NP 1628

14. Mon. Monday of the 2nd Week of Lent
    ALL 157, Ps 1236; NP 1632

15. Tue. Tuesday of the 2nd Week of Lent
    ALL 166, Ps 1257; NP 1635

16. Wed. Wednesday of the 2nd Week of Lent
    ALL 175, Ps 1278; NP 1638

17. Thu. Thursday of the 2nd Week of Lent
    OOR 184, Ps 1302 (May add Rd & Pr of St. Patrick, B 1710-1712)
    MP 188, Ps 1306 (May add Ant & Pr of St. Patrick 1712)
    DP 189, Ps 1311
    EP 190, Ps 1316 (May add Ant 1713 & Pr of St. Patrick 1712)
    NP 1642

18. Fri. Friday of the 2nd Week of Lent
    OOR 192, Ps 1322 (May add Rd & Pr of St. Cyril of Jerusalem, B & D
        1713-1715)
    MP 197, Pr 1325 (May add Ant & Pr of St. Cyril 1715)
    DP 198, Ps 1330
    EP I (of St. Joseph) 1716; NP 1625

19. Sat. ST. JOSEPH, HUSBAND OF MARY (Sol)
    ALL 1719, Te Deum; DP Ps 1651
    EP I (of Sunday) 208, Ps 1355; NP 1625

20. **Sun. THIRD SUNDAY OF LENT**
    ALL 210, Ps 1360; NP 1628

21. Mon. Monday of the 3rd Week of Lent
    ALL 221, Ps 1379; NP1632

22. Tue. Tuesday of the 3rd Week of Lent
    ALL 228, Ps 1397; NP 1635

23. Wed. Wednesday of the 3rd Week of Lent
    OOR 237, Ps 1416 (May add Rd & Pr of St. Turibius de Mogrovejo, B
        1730-1732)

MP 242, Ps 1421 (May add Ant & Pr of St. Turibius 1732)
DP 243, Ps 1426
EP 245, Ps 1430 (May add Ant 1733 & Pr of St. Turibius 1732); NP 1638

24.   Thu. Thursday of the 3rd Week of Lent
ALL 246, Ps 1435
EP I (of Annunciation) 1733; NP 1625

25.   Fri. ANNUNCIATION OF THE LORD (Sol)
ALL 1738, Te Deum; DP Ps 1651; NP 1628

26.   Sat. Saturday of the 3rd Week of Lent
ALL 263, Ps 1472
EP I (of Sunday) 271, Ps 1486; NP 1625

27.   **Sun. FOURTH SUNDAY OF LENT**
ALL 273, Ps 1491; NP 1628

28.   Mon. Monday of the 4th Week of Lent
ALL 283, Ps 1512; NP 1632

29.   Tue. Tuesday of the 4th Week of Lent
ALL 292, Ps 1532; NP 1635

30.   Wed. Wednesday of the 4th Week of Lent
ALL 301, Ps 1551; NP 1638

31.   Thu. Thursday of the 4th Week of Lent
ALL 311, Ps 1571; NP 1642

APRIL

1.   Fri. Friday of the 4th Week of Lent
ALL 320, Ps 1588; NP 1644

2.   Sat. Saturday of the 4th Week of Lent
OOR 328, Ps 1607 (May add Rd & Pr of St. Francis of Paola, Hermit 1757-1759)
MP 333, Ps 1611 (May add Ant & Pr of St. Francis 1759)
DP 334, Ps 1615
EP I (of Sunday) 336, Ps 1076; NP 1625

3.   **Sun. FIFTH SUNDAY OF LENT**
ALL 338, Ps 1082; NP 1628

4.   Mon. Monday of the 5th Week of Lent
OOR 348, Ps 1102 (May add Rd & Pr of St. Isidore, B & D 1760-1762)
MP 352, Ps 1107 (May add Ant & Pr of St. Isidore 1762)

DP 354, Ps 1111
EP 355, Ps 1115 (May add Ant & Pr of St. Isidore 1762); NP 1632

5. Tue. Tuesday of the 5th Week of Lent
OOR 356, Ps 1121 (May add Rd & Pr of St. Vincent Ferrer, P 1763-1764)
MP 360, Ps 1126 (May add Ant & Pr of St. Vincent 1764)
DP 362, Ps 1131
EP 363, Ps 1135 (May add Ant & Pr of St. Vincent 1764); NP 1635

6. Wed. Wednesday of the 5th Week of Lent
ALL 365, Ps 1141; NP 1638

7. Thu. Thursday of the 5th Week of Lent
OOR 373, Ps 1158 (May add Rd & Pr of St. John Baptist de la Salle, P 1765-1767)
MP 376, Ps 1162 (May add Ant & Pr of St. John 1767)
DP 378, Ps 1167
EP 379, Ps 1171 (May add Ant & Pr of St. John 1767); NP 1642

8. Fri. Friday of the 5th Week of Lent
ALL 381, Ps 1176; NP 1644

9. Sat. Saturday of the 5th Week of Lent
ALL 390, Ps 1194
EP I (of Sunday) 413, Ps 1208; NP 1625
Hymns during Holy Week 398-412

10. **Sun. PASSION SUNDAY (PALM SUNDAY)**
ALL 416, Ps 1214; NP 1628

11. Mon. Monday of Holy Week
ALL 430, Hymn 403; Ps 1236; NP 1632

12. Tue. Tuesday of Holy Week
ALL 439, Hymn 403; Ps 1257; NP 1635

13. Wed. Wednesday of Holy Week
ALL 447, Hymn 403; Ps 1278; NP 1638

14. Thu. HOLY THURSDAY
OOR 457, Hymn 403; Ps 1302 or 1454
MP 460, Hymn 408; Ps 1306; DP 462, Ps 1311
EP (if absent from Lord's Supper) 464, Ps 1316
NP 1628, proper Ant instead of Responsory

15. Fri. GOOD FRIDAY
    ALL 467, EP (if absent from Lord's Passion) 487
    NP 1628, proper Ant instead of Responsory

16. Sat. HOLY SATURDAY
    ALL 492, EP 509
    NP (if absent from Easter Vigil) 1628, proper Ant
    Hymns for Easter Season 536-548

17. **Sun. EASTER SUNDAY**
    OOR (if absent from Easter Vigil) 515, Te Deum
    MP 524, Invitatory, Ps 1087; DP 526, Hymn 546
    EP 531, Hymn 536
    NP 1625 or 1628, Hymn 540, Ant instead of Responsory 541

18. Mon. MONDAY WITHIN THE OCTAVE OF EASTER
    OOR 549, Te Deum; MP 556, Hymn, etc. 524
    DP 557, Hymn 546; EP 561, Hymn, etc. 531
    NP 1625 or 1628, Hymn 540, Ant instead of Responsory 541

19. Tue. TUESDAY WITHIN THE OCTAVE OF EASTER
    OOR 563, Te Deum; MP 570, Hymn, etc. 524
    DP 571, Hymn 546; EP 575, Hymn, etc. 531
    NP 1625 or 1628, Hymn 540, Ant instead of Responsory 541

20. Wed. WEDNESDAY WITHIN THE OCTAVE OF EASTER
    OOR 577, Te Deum; MP 584, Hymn, etc. 524
    DP 586, Hymn 546; EP 589, Hymn, etc. 531
    NP 1625 or 1628, Hymn 540, Ant instead of Responsory 541

21. Thu. THURSDAY WITHIN THE OCTAVE OF EASTER
    OOR 591, Te Deum; MP 598, Hymn, etc. 524
    DP 599, Hymn 546; EP 603, Hymn, etc. 531
    NP 1625 or 1628, Hymn 540, Ant instead of Responsory 541

22. Fri. FRIDAY WITHIN THE OCTAVE OF EASTER
    OOR 604, Te Deum; MP 610, Hymn, etc. 524
    DP 612, Hymn 546; EP 615, Hymn, etc. 531
    NP 1625 or 1628, Hymn 540, Ant instead of Responsory 541

23. Sat. SATURDAY WITHIN THE OCTAVE OF EASTER
    OOR 617, Te Deum
    MP 623, Hymn, etc. 524; DP 624, Hymn 546
    EP I (of Sunday) 629, Hymn, etc. 531
    NP 1625 or 1628, Hymn 540, Ant instead of Responsory 541

24. Sun. **SECOND SUNDAY OF EASTER**
    OOR 631, Te Deum
    MP 637, Hymn, etc. 524; DP 526, Pr 638
    EP 639, Hymn, etc. 531; NP 1628

25. Mon. ST. MARK, EVANGELIST (F) (1782)
    From Com of Ap in Easter 1951 and Proper; Te Deum
    DP 1246, Rd, etc. 1788, Pr 1787; NP 1632

26. Tue. Tuesday of the 2nd Week of Easter
    OOR 650, Hymn 542, Ps 1257
    MP 654, Hymn 544, Ps 1263; DP 655, Hymn 546, Ps 1268
    EP 656, Hymn 536, Ps 1272; NP 1635, Hymn 540

27. Wed. Wednesday of the 2nd Week of Easter
    ALL 658, Ps 1278; NP 1638

28. Thu. Thursday of the 2nd Week of Easter
    ALL 666, Ps 1302; NP 1642

OR: St. Peter Chanel, P & M (1791)
    From Com of M in Easter 2015
    OOR 1301, Rd 666 & 1791, Pr 1793
    MP 2024, Ps 1306, Pr 1793; DP 672, Ps 1311
    EP 2035, Ps 1316, Pr 1793; NP 1642

OR: St. Louis Grignion de Montfort, P *(New)*
    From Com of Pas 2052
    OOR 1301, Rd 666 & 2059, Pr 2075
    MP 2070, Ps 1306, Pr as above; DP 672, Ps 1311
    EP 2077, Ps 1316, Pr as above; NP 1642

29. Fri. St. Catherine of Siena, V & D (Mem) (1793)
    From Com of V 2104
    OOR 1321, Rd 675 & 1794, Pr 1796
    MP 2114, Ps 1325, Ant 1795 & Pr 1796; DP 680, Ps 1330
    EP 2120, Ps 1334, Ant & Pr 1796; NP 1644

30. Sat. Saturday of the 2nd Week of Easter
    ALL 683, Ps 1340; EP see below

OR: St. Pius V, Po (1796)
    From Com of Pas 2052
    OOR 1339, Rd 683 & 1796, Pr 1798
    MP 2070, Ps 1345, Pr 1798; DP 688, Ps 1350
    EP I (of Sunday) 690, Ps 1355; NP 1625

MAY

1. **Sun. THIRD SUNDAY OF EASTER**
   ALL 692, Ps 1360, Te Deum; NP 1628

2. Mon. St. Athanasius, B & D (Mem) (1807)
   From Com of Pas 2052 or D 2086
   OOR 1379, Rd 702 & 1808, Pr 1810
   MP from Com, Ps 1383, Pr 1810; DP 707, Ps 1388
   EP from Com, Ps 1392, Pr 1810; NP 1632

3. Tue. STS. PHILIP AND JAMES, AP (F) (1810)
   From Com of Ap in Easter 1951 and Proper; Te Deum
   DP 1407, Rd, etc. 1962, Pr 1814; NP 1635

4. Wed. Wednesday of the 3rd Week of Easter
   ALL 718, Ps 1416; NP 1638

5. Thu. Thursday of the 3rd Week of Easter
   ALL 726, Ps 1435; NP 1642

6. Fri. Friday of the 3rd Week of Easter
   ALL 733, Ps 1454; NP 1644

7. Sat. Saturday of the 3rd Week of Easter
   ALL 741, Ps 1472
   EP I (of Sunday) 748, Ps 1486; NP 1625

8. **Sun. FOURTH SUNDAY OF EASTER**
   ALL 750, Ps 1491, Te Deum; NP 1628

9. Mon. Monday of the 4th Week of Easter
   ALL 760, Ps 1512; NP 1632

10. Tue. Tuesday of the 4th Week of Easter
    ALL 768, Ps 1532; NP 1635

OR: St. Damien de Veuster of Molokai, P *(New)*
    OOR 1531, Rd 768 & 2068, Pr proper or 2075
    MP 2070, Ps 1537, Pr as above; DP 774, Ps 1541
    EP 2077, Ps 1545, Pr as above; NP 1635

11. Wed. Wednesday of the 4th Week of Easter
    ALL 777, Ps 1551; NP 1638

12. Thu. Thursday of the 4th Week of Easter
    ALL 785, Ps 1571; NP 1642

OR: Sts. Nereus and Achilleus, Mm (1817)
    From Com of Mm in Easter 1977

OOR 1570, Rd 785 & 1817, Pr 1819
MP 1987, Ps 1574, Pr 1819; DP 791, Ps 1579
EP 1997, Ps 1583, Pr 1819; NP 1642

OR: St. Pancras, M (1819)
From Com of M in Easter 2015
OOR 1570, Rd 785 & 1820, Pr 1821
MP 2024, Ps 1574, Pr 1821; DP 791, Ps 1579
EP 2035, Ps 1583, Pr 1821; NP 1642

13. Fri. Friday of the 4th Week of Easter
ALL 794, Ps 1588; NP 1644

OR: Our Lady of Fatima *(New)*
OOR 1587, Rd 794 & 1926f, Pr 1937
MP 1931, Ps 1593, Pr 1937; DP 800, Ps 1598
EP 1940, Ps 1601, Pr 1937; NP 1644

14. Sat. ST. MATTHIAS, AP (F) (1822)
From Com of Ap in Easter 1951 and Proper, Te Deum
DP 1615, Rd, etc. 1962, Pr 1825
EP I (of Sunday) 811, Ps 1076; NP 1625

15. **Sun. FIFTH SUNDAY OF EASTER**
ALL 813, Ps 1082, Te Deum; NP 1628

16. Mon. Monday of the 5th Week of Easter
ALL 823, Ps 1102; NP 1632

17. Tue. Tuesday of the 5th Week of Easter
ALL 831, Ps 1121; NP 1635

18. Wed. Wednesday of the 5th Week of Easter
ALL 839, Ps 1141; NP 1638

OR: St. John I, Po & M (1825)
From Com of M in Easter 2015 or Pas 2052
OOR 1140, Rd 839 & 1826, Pr 1828
MP from Com, Ps 1146, Pr 1828; DP 844, Ps 1150
EP from Com, Ps 1153, Pr 1828; NP 1638

19. Thu. Thursday of the 5th Week of Easter
ALL 847, Ps 1158; NP 1642

20. Fri. Friday of the 5th Week of Easter
ALL 854, Ps 1176; NP 1644

OR: St. Bernardine of Siena, P (1828)
From Com of Pas 2052

OOR 1176, Rd 855 & 1828, Pr 1830
MP 2070, Ps 1180, Pr 1830; DP 859, Ps 1185
EP 2077, Ps 1190, Pr 1830; NP 1644

21. Sat. Saturday of the 5th Week of Easter
ALL 862, Ps 1194; EP see below

OR: St. Christopher Magallanes, P, and Comps, Mm *(New)*
From Com of Mm in Easter, 1977
OOR 1194, Rd 862 & 1984, Pr 1993
MP 1987, Ps 1200, Pr 1993; DP 867, Ps 1203
EP I (of Sunday) 869, Ps 1208; NP 1625

22. **Sun. SIXTH SUNDAY OF EASTER**
ALL 871, Ps 1214, Te Deum; NP 1628

23. Mon. Monday of the 6th Week of Easter
ALL 880, Ps 1236; NP 1632

24. Tue. Tuesday of the 6th Week of Easter
ALL 888, Ps 1257; NP 1635

25. Wed. Wednesday of the 6th Week of Easter
ALL 896, Ps 1278; EP see below

OR: Venerable Bede, P & D (1831)
From Com of D 2086 or Rel 2195
OOR 1277, Rd 896 & 1831, Pr 1833
MP from Com, Ps 1284, Pr 1833; DP 901, Ps 1290
EP see below

OR: St. Gregory VII, Po (1833)
From Com of Pas 2052
OOR 1277, Rd 896 & 1834, Pr 1835
MP 2070, Ps 1284, Pr 1835; DP 901, Ps 1290
EP see below

OR: St. Mary Magdalene de Pazzi (1836)
From Com of V 2104 or Rel 2195
OOR 1277, Rd 896 & 1836, Pr 1838
MP from Com, Ps 1284, Pr 1838; DP 901, Ps 1290
EP I (of Ascension) 909; NP 1625

26. **Thu. ASCENSION (Sol)**
ALL 914, Te Deum; NP 1628

27. Fri. Friday of the 6th Week of Easter
ALL 935, Ps 1322; NP 1644

OR: St. Augustine of Canterbury, B (1841)
From Com of Pas 2052
OOR 1321, Rd 935 & 1841, Pr 1843
MP 2070, Ps 1325, Pr 1843; DP 942, Ps 1330
EP 2077, Ps 1334, Pr 1843; NP 1644

28. Sat. Saturday of the 6th Week of Easter
ALL 946, Ps 1340
EP I (of Sunday) 954, Ps 1355; NP 1625

29. **Sun. SEVENTH SUNDAY OF EASTER**
ALL 956, Ps 1360, Te Deum; NP 1628

WHERE THE ASCENSION IS NOT TO BE OBSERVED AS A HOLYDAY OF OBLIGATION, IT IS ASSIGNED TO THE SEVENTH SUNDAY OF EASTER. **The specified rubrics below are to be followed until Monday of the 7th Week of Easter.**

25. Wed. Wednesday of the 6th Week of Easter
ALL 896, Ps 1278; EP 902; NP 1638

OR: Venerable Bede, P & D (1831)
From Com of D 2086 or Rel 2195
OOR 1277, Rd 896 & 1831, Pr 1833
MP from Com, Ps 1284, Pr 1833; DP 901, Ps 1290
EP from Com, Ps 1295, Pr 1833; NP 1638

OR: St. Gregory VII, Po (1833)
From Com of Pas 2052
OOR 1277, Rd 896 & 1834, Pr 1835
MP 2070, Ps 1284, Pr 1835; DP 901, Ps 1290
EP 2077, Ps 1295, Pr 1835; NP 1638

OR: St. Mary Magdalene de Pazzi (1836)
From Com of V 2104 or Rel 2195
OOR 1277, Rd 896 & 1836, Pr 1838
MP from Com, Ps 1284, Pr 1838; DP 901, Ps 1290
EP from Com, Ps 1295, Pr 1838; NP 1638

26. Thu. St. Philip Neri, P (Mem) (1838)
From Com of Pas 2052 or Rel 2195
OOR 1301, Verse, Rd & Resp 935 **(from Fri.)** & 1839, Pr 1841
MP from Com, Ps 1306, Pr 1841; DP 906, Ps 1311
EP from Com, Ps 1316, Pr 1841; NP 1642

27. Fri. Friday of the 6th Week of Easter
ALL 935, Ps 1322, Verse, Rd & Resp 946 **(from Sat.)**; NP 1644

OR: St. Augustine of Canterbury, B (1841)
From Com of Pas 2052
OOR 1321, Verse, Rd & Resp 946 **(from Sat.)** & 1841, Pr 1843
MP 2070, Ps 1325, Pr 1843; DP 942, Ps 1330
EP 2077, Ps 1334, Pr 1843; NP 1644

28. Sat. Saturday of the 6th Week of Easter
ALL 946, Ps 1340, Verse, Rd & Resp 956 **(from Sun.)**
EP I (of Ascension) 909; NP 1625

29. **Sun. ASCENSION (Sol)**
All 914, Te Deum; NP 1628

30. Mon. Monday of the 7th Week of Easter
ALL 965, Ps 1379; NP 1632

31. Tue. VISITATION (F) (1844)
ALL 1844 & from Com of BVM 1917; Te Deum
DP 978, Rd, etc. 1850; NP 1635

JUNE

1. Wed. St. Justin, M (Mem) (1854)
From Com of M in Easter 2015
OOR 1415, Rd 981 & 1854, Pr 1857
MP 2024, Ps 1421, Ant & Pr 1857; DP 986, Ps 1426
EP 2035, Ps 1430, Ant & Pr 1857; NP 1638

2. Thu. Thursday of the 7th Week of Easter
ALL 989, Ps 1435; NP 1642

OR: Sts. Marcellinus and Peter, Mm (1857)
From Com of Mm in Easter 1977
OOR 1435, Rd 989 & 1858, Pr 1860
MP 1987, Ps 1440, Pr 1860; DP 993, Ps 1445
EP 1997, Ps 1450, Pr 1860; NP 1642

3. Fri. St. Charles Lwanga and Comps, Mm (Mem) (1860)
From Com of M in Easter 1977
OOR 1454, Rd 996 & 1860, Pr 1862
MP 1987, Ps 1459, Pr 1862; DP 1001, Ps 1463
EP 1997, Ps 1468, Pr 1862; NP 1644

4. Sat. Saturday of the 7th Week of Easter
ALL 1004, Ps 1472
EP I (of Pentecost) 1011; NP 1625

5. **Sun. PENTECOST (Sol)**
   ALL 1017, Te Deum; NP 1628

RETURN TO VOLUME III

6. Mon. The Blessed Virgin Mary, Mother of the Church (Mem) *(New)*
   From Com of BVM 1614
   OOR 847, Rd 322 & 1621f, Pr p. 47 of this Guide
   MP 1626, Ps 853, Pr p. 47 of this Guide; DP 858
   EP 1634, Ps 864, Pr p. 47 of this Guide; NP 1275

7. Tue. Tuesday of the 10th Week in Ordinary Time
   ALL 869, Rd 326 & Pr 330; NP 1278

8. Wed. Wednesday of the 10th Week in Ordinary Time
   ALL 891, Rd 331 & Pr 335; NP 1280

9. Thu. Thursday of the 10th Week in Ordinary Time
   ALL 916, Rd 336 & Pr 340; NP 1283

OR: St. Ephrem, De & D (1460)
   From Com of D 1763
   OOR 916, Rd 336 & 1460, Pr 1462
   MP 1768, Ps 920, Pr 1462; DP 926
   EP 1770, Ps 932, Pr 1462; NP 1283

10. Fri. Friday of the 10th Week in Ordinary Time
    ALL 937, Rd 340 & Pr 344; NP 1285

11. Sat. St. Barnabas, Ap (Mem) (1462)
    From Com of Ap and Proper; Invit 1463
    OOR Hymn 1659, Ps 959, Rd 345 & 1463, Pr 1466
    MP Hymn 1666, Ps 962, Rd, etc. 1465; DP 968, Rd, etc. 1467
    EP I (of Trinity Sunday) 573; NP 1269

12. **Sun. TRINITY SUNDAY (Sol)**
    ALL 578, Te Deum; DP Ps 693; NP 1272

13. Mon. St. Anthony of Padua, P & D (Mem) (1469)
    From Com of Pas 1734 or D 1763 or Rel 1858
    OOR 998, Rd 355 & 1470, Pr 1471
    MP from Com, Ps 1002, Pr 1471; DP 1007
    EP from Com, Ps 1012, Pr 1471; NP 1275

14. Tue. Tuesday of the 11th Week in Ordinary Time
    ALL 1018, Rd 360 & Pr 364; NP 1278

15. Wed. Wednesday of the 11th Week in Ordinary Time
ALL 1039, Rd 364 & Pr 368; NP 1280

16. Thu. Thursday of the 11th Week in Ordinary Time
ALL 1061, Rd 369 & Pr 373; NP 1283

17. Fri. Friday of the 11th Week in Ordinary Time
ALL 1082, Rd 373 & Pr 378; NP 1285

18. Sat. Saturday of the 11th Week in Ordinary Time
ALL 1103, Rd 378 & Pr 382; EP see below

OR: BVM on Saturday - 1642 & 1103
Rd 378 & 1642f, Pr 1653f; DP 1112
EP I (of Corpus Christi) 597; NP 1269

19. **Sun. CORPUS CHRISTI (Sol)**
ALL 604, Te Deum; DP Ps 693; NP 1272

20. Mon. Monday of the 12th Week in Ordinary Time
ALL 1143, Rd 388 & Pr 392; NP 1275

21. Tue. St. Aloysius Gonzaga, Rel (Mem) (1474)
From Com of Rel 1858
OOR 1165, Rd 393 & 1474, Pr 1476
MP 1862, Ps 1170, Pr 1476; DP 1176
EP 1864, Ps 1181, Pr 1476; NP 1278

22. Wed. Wednesday of the 12th Week in Ordinary Time
All 1187, Rd 397 & Pr 401; EP see below

OR: St. Paulinus of Nola, B (1476)
From Com of Pas 1734
OOR 1187, Rd 397 & 1477, Pr 1479
MP 1749, Ps 1192, Pr 1479; DP 1197; EP see below

OR: Sts. John Fisher, B & M, and Thomas More, M (1479)
From Com of Mm 1680
OOR 1187, Rd 397 & 1479, Pr 1481
MP 1688, Ps 1192, Pr 1481; DP 1197
EP I (of St. John the Baptist) 1482; NP 1269

23. Thu. BIRTH OF ST. JOHN THE BAPTIST (Sol)
ALL 1485, Te Deum; DP Ps 1291
EP I (of Sacred Heart) 624; NP 1269

24. Fri. SACRED HEART (Sol)
ALL 629, Te Deum; DP Ps 1291; NP 1272

25. Sat. Immaculate Heart of BVM (Mem) (1444)
From Com of BVM 1614
OOR 1250, Rd 410 & 1444, Pr 1446
MP 1626, Ps 1254, Ant & Pr 1446; DP 1259
EP I (of Sunday) 677, Ant & Pr 415; NP 1269

26. **Sun. THIRTEENTH SUNDAY IN ORDINARY TIME**
ALL 682, Rd, Te Deum, Ant & Pr 415; NP 1272

27. Mon. Monday of the 13th Week in Ordinary Time
ALL 702, Rd 420 & Pr 424; NP 1275

OR: St. Cyril of Alexandria, B & D (1495)
From Com of Pas 1734 or D 1763
OOR 702, Rd 420 & 1496, Pr 1497
MP from Com, Ps 706, Pr 1497; DP 711
EP from Com, Ps 717, Pr 1497; NP 1275

28. Tue. St. Irenaeus, B & M (Mem) (1498)
From Com of M 1707 or Pas 1734
OOR 722, Rd 425 & 1498, Pr 1500
MP from Com, Ps 728, Ant & Pr 1500; DP 733
EP I (of Sts. Peter and Paul) 1500; NP 1269

29. Wed. STS. PETER AND PAUL, AP (Sol)
ALL 1503, Te Deum; DP 1291; NP 1272

30. Thu. Thursday of the 13th Week in Ordinary Time
ALL 765, Rd 433 & Pr 437; NP 1283

OR: First Martyrs of the Church of Rome (1513)
From Com of Mm 1680
OOR 765, Rd 433 & 1513, Pr 1515
MP 1688, Ps 769, Ant & Pr 1515; DP 774
EP 1694, Ps 780, Ant & Pr 1515; NP 1283

JULY

1. Fri. Friday of the 13th Week in Ordinary Time
ALL 786, Rd 438 & Pr 442; NP 1285

OR: St. Junipero Serra, P **(New)** (8)
From Com of Pas 1734
OOR 786, Rd 438 or 1745, Pr proper (8) or 1753
MP 1749, Ps 790, Pr (8); DP 796
EP 1755, Ps 802, Pr (8); NP 1285

2. Sat. Saturday of the 13th Week in Ordinary Time
ALL 807, Rd 442 & Pr 446; EP see below

OR: BVM on Saturday - 1642 & 807
Rd 442 & 1642f, Pr 1653f; DP 816
EP I (of Sunday) 821, Ant & Pr 447; NP 1269

3. **Sun. FOURTEENTH SUNDAY IN ORDINARY TIME**
ALL 826, Rd, Te Deum, Ant & Pr 447; NP 1272

4. Mon. Monday of the 14th Week in Ordinary Time
ALL 847, Rd 453 & Pr 457; NP 1275

5. Tue. Tuesday of the 14th Week in Ordinary Time
ALL 869, Rd 457 & Pr 462; NP 1278

OR: St. Anthony Zaccaria, P (1523)
From Com of Pas 1734 or Tea 1871 or Rel 1858
OOR 869, Rd 457 & 1523, Pr 1525
MP from Com, Ps 875, Pr 1525; DP 881
EP from Com, Ps 886, Pr 1525; NP 1278

OR: St. Elizabeth of Portugal (1520) **[transferred from July 4]**
From Com of HW (Underpriv) 1866
OOR 869, Rd 457 & 1521, Pr 1522
MP 1843, Ps 875, Ant 1869, Pr 1522; DP 881
EP 1849, Ps 886, Ant 1870, Pr 1522, NP 1278

6. Wed. Wednesday of the 14th Week in Ordinary Time
ALL 891, Rd 462 & Pr 466; NP 1280

OR: St. Maria Goretti, V & M (1525)
From Com of M 1707 or V 1777
OOR 891, Rd 462 & 1525, Pr 1527
MP from Com, Ps 897, Pr 1527; DP 903
EP from Com, Ps 910, Pr 1527; NP 1280

7. Thu. Thursday of the 14th Week in Ordinary Time
ALL 916, Rd 467 & Pr 470; NP 1283

8. Fri. Friday of the 14th Week in Ordinary Time
ALL 937, Rd 471 & Pr 475; NP 1285

9. Sat. Saturday of the 14th Week in Ordinary Time
ALL 958, Rd 475 & Pr 478; EP see below

OR: St. Augustine Zhao Rong, P, and Comps, Mm *(New)*
From Com of Mm 1680

OOR 958, Rd 475 & 1686, Pr 1692
MP 1688, Ps 962, Ant 1691 & Pr 1692; DP 968; EP see below

OR: BVM on Saturday - 1642 & 958
Rd 475 & 1642f, Pr 1653f; DP 968
EP I (of Sunday) 973, Ant & Pr 480; NP 1269

10. Sun. **FIFTEENTH SUNDAY IN ORDINARY TIME**
ALL 978, Rd, Te Deum, Ant & Pr 480; NP 1272

11. Mon. St. Benedict, Ab (Mem) (1527)
From Com of Rel 1858
OOR 998, Rd 485 & 1528, Pr 1530
MP 1862, Ps 1002, Ant & Pr 1530; DP 1007
EP 1864, Ps 1012, Ant & Pr 1530; NP 1275

12. Tue. Tuesday of the 15th Week in Ordinary Time
ALL 1018, Rd 489 & Pr 494; NP 1278

13. Wed. Wednesday of the 15th Week in Ordinary Time
ALL 1039, Rd 494 & Pr 499; NP 1280

OR: St. Henry (1531)
From Com of HM 1804
OOR 1039, Rd 494 & 1531, Pr 1533
MP 1815, Ps 1045, Pr 1533; DP 1050
EP 1822, Ps 1056, Pr 1533; NP 1280

14. Thu. St. Kateri Tekakwitha, V (Mem) **(New)** (9)
From Com of V 1777
OOR 1061, Rd 499 & 1782, Pr proper (9) or 1789
MP 1786, Ps 1066, Pr proper (9) or 1789; DP 1071
EP 1791, Ps 1077, Pr proper (9) or 1797; NP 1283

15. Fri. St. Bonaventure, B & D (Mem) (1535)
From Com of Pas 1734 or D 1763
OOR 1082, Rd 504 & 1535, Pr 1537
MP from Com, Ps 1087, Pr 1537; DP 1092
EP from Com, Ps 1098, Pr 1537; NP 1285

16. Sat. Saturday of the 15th Week in Ordinary Time
ALL 1103, Rd 509 & Pr 513; EP see below

OR: Our Lady of Mount Carmel (1538)
From Com of BVM 1614
OOR 1103, Rd 509 & 1538, Pr 1540
MP 1626, Ps 1108, Ant & Pr 1540; DP 1112; EP see below

OR: BVM on Saturday - 1642 & 1103
Rd 509 & 1642f, Pr 1653f; DP 1112
EP I (of Sunday) 1117, Ant & Pr 514; NP 1269

17. **Sun. SIXTEENTH SUNDAY IN ORDINARY TIME**
ALL 1122, Rd, Te Deum, Ant & Pr 514; NP 1272

18. Mon. Monday of the 16th Week in Ordinary Time
ALL 1143, Rd 518 & Pr 522; NP 1275

OR: St. Camillus de Lellis, P (1533) **[transferred from 7/14]**
From Com of HM (Underpriv) 1866
OOR 1143, Rd 518 & 1533, Pr 1535
MP 1815, Ps 1148, Ant 1869, Pr 1535; DP 1154
EP 1822, Ps 1160, Ant 1870, Pr 1535; NP 1275

19. Tue. Tuesday of the 16th Week in Ordinary Week
ALL 1165, Rd 522 & Pr 525; NP 1278

20. Wed. Wednesday of the 16th Week in Ordinary Week
ALL 1187, Rd 526 & Pr 529; NP 1280

OR: St. Apollinarius, B & M *(New)*
From Com of M 1707 or Pas 1734
OOR 1187, Rd 526 & 1712, Pr 1719 or 1752
MP from Com, Ps 1192, Pr 1719 or 1752; DP 1197
EP from Com, Ps 1204, Pr 1719 or 1752; NP 1280

21. Thu. Thursday of the 16th Week in Ordinary Time
ALL 1210, Rd 529 & Pr 532; NP 1283

OR: St. Lawrence of Brindisi, P & D (1540)
From Com of Pas 1734 or D 1763
OOR 1210, Rd 529 & 1541, Pr 1542
MP from Com, Ps 1214, Pr 1542; DP 1219
EP from Com, Ps 1225, Pr 1542; NP 1283

22. Fri. St. Mary Magdalene (F) (1543)
From Com of HW 1835 and Proper, Te Deum
DP 1240, Rd, etc. 1848, Pr 1546; NP 1285

23. Sat. Saturday of the 16th Week in Ordinary Time
ALL 1250, Rd 537 & Pr 540; EP see below

OR: St. Bridget, Rel (1547)
From Com of Rel 1858
OOR 1250, Rd 537 & 1548, Pr 1550
MP 1862, Ps 1254, Pr 1550; DP 1259; EP see below

OR: BVM on Saturday - 1642 & 1250
Rd 537 & 1642f, Pr 1653f; DP 1259
EP I (of Sunday) 677, Ant & Pr 541; NP 1269

24. Sun. **SEVENTEENTH SUNDAY IN ORDINARY TIME**
ALL 682, Rd, Te Deum, Ant & Pr 541; NP 1272

25. Mon. ST. JAMES, AP (F) (1551)
From Com of Ap 1659 and Proper, Te Deum
DP 711, Rd, etc. 1668, Pr 1554; NP 1275

26. Tue. Sts. Joachim and Ann, Parents of Mary (Mem) (1555)
From Com of HM 1804
OOR 722, Rd 549 & 1556, Pr 1558
MP Hymn 1815, Ps 728, Rd, etc.1557; DP 733
EP Hymn 1822, Ps 739, Rd, etc. 1559; NP 1278

27. Wed. Wednesday of the 17th Week in Ordinary Time
ALL 744, Rd 553 & Pr 557; NP 1280

28. Thu. Thursday of the 17th Week in Ordinary Time
ALL 765, Rd 558 & Pr 561; NP 1283

29. Fri. St. Martha (Mem) (1559)
From Com of HW 1835
OOR 786, Rd 562 & 1560, Pr 1562
MP Hymn 1843, Ps 790, Ant & Pr 1562; DP 796
EP Hymn 1849, Ps 802, Ant & Pr 1562; NP 1285

30. Sat. Saturday of the 17th Week in Ordinary Time
ALL 807, Rd 566 & Pr 570; EP see next volume (IV)

OR: St. Peter Chrysologus, B & D (1562)
From Com of Pas 1734 or D 1763
OOR 807, Rd 566 & 1563, Pr 1564
MP from Com, Ps 811, Pr 1564; DP 816
EP see next volume (IV)

OR: BVM on Saturday - 1642 & 807
Rd 566 & 1642f, Pr 1653f; DP 816

BEGIN VOLUME IV

EP I (of Sunday) 785, Ant & Pr 53; NP 1233

31. Sun. **EIGHTEENTH SUNDAY IN ORDINARY TIME**
ALL 790, Rd, Te Deum, Ant & Pr 53; NP 1236

AUGUST

1. Mon. St. Alphonsus Liguori, B & D (Mem) (1264)
   From Com of Pas 1748 or D 1777
   OOR 811, Rd 59 & 1264, Pr 1266
   MP from Com, Ps 817, Pr 1266; DP 822
   EP from Com, Ps 828, Pr 1266; NP 1239

2. Tue. Tuesday of the 18th Week in Ordinary Time
   ALL 833, Rd 63 & Pr 68; NP 1242

OR: St. Eusebius of Vercelli, B (1266)
   From Com of Pas 1748
   OOR 833, Rd 63 & 1266, Pr 1268
   MP 1763, Ps 839, Pr 1268; DP 845
   EP 1769, Ps 850, Pr 1268; NP 1242

OR: St. Peter Julian Eymard, P *(New)*
   From Com of Pas 1748 or Rel 1872
   OOR 833, Rd 63 & 1759 or 1874, Pr proper or 1767 or 1878
   MP from Com, Ps 839, Pr as above; DP 845
   EP from Com, Ps 850, Pr as above; NP 1242

3. Wed. Wednesday of the 18th Week in Ordinary Time
   ALL 855, Rd 68 & Pr 72; NP 1244

4. Thu. St. John Vianney, P (Mem) (1268)
   From Com of Pas 1748
   OOR 880, Rd 73 & 1269, Pr 1271
   MP 1763, Ps 884, Pr 1271; DP 890
   EP 1769, Ps 896, Pr 1271; NP 1247

5. Fri. Friday of the 18th Week in Ordinary Time
   ALL 901, Rd 78 & Pr 83; NP 1249

OR: Dedication of Saint Mary Major (1271)
   From Com of BVM 1628
   OOR 901, Rd 78 & 1271, Pr 1273
   MP 1640, Ps 905, Ant & Pr 1273; DP 910
   EP 1648, Ps 916, Ant 1274 & Pr 1273; NP 1249

6. Sat. TRANSFIGURATION (F)
   ALL 1278, Te Deum; DP Ps 932
   EP I (of Sunday) 937, Ant & Pr 88; NP 1233

7. Sun. **NINETEENTH SUNDAY IN ORDINARY TIME**
   ALL 942, Rd, Te Deum, Ant & Pr 88; NP 1236

8. Mon. St. Dominic, P (Mem) (1301)
From Com of Pas 1748 or Rel 1872
OOR 962, Rd 92 & 1301, Pr 1303
MP from Com, Ps 966, Pr 1303; DP 971
EP from Com, Ps 976, Pr 1303; NP 1239

9. Tue. Tuesday of the 19th Week in Ordinary Time
ALL 982, Rd 96 & Pr 100; NP 1242

OR: St. Teresa Benedicta of the Cross, V & M (Edith Stein) *(New)*
From Com of M 1721 or V 1791
OOR 982, Rd 96 & 1726f or 1796f, Pr 1733
MP from Com, Ps 988, Pr 1733; DP 993
EP from Com, Ps 998, Pr 1733; NP 1242

10. Wed. ST. LAWRENCE, DE & M (F) (1303)
From Com of M 1721 and Proper, Te Deum
DP 1014, Rd, etc. 1734, Pr 1308; NP 1244

11. Thu. St. Clare, V (Mem) (1310)
From Com of V 1791 or Rel 1872
OOR 1025, Rd 104 & 1310, Pr 1312
MP from Com, Ps 1030, Pr 1312; DP 1035
EP from Com, Ps 1041, Pr 1312; NP 1247

12. Fri. Friday of the 19th Week in Ordinary Time
ALL 1046, Rd 108 & Pr 112; NP 1249

OR: St. Jane Frances de Chantal, Rel **(New)** (14) or see Vol. I, 1240
From Com of Rel 1872 **[transferred from 8/18]**
OOR 1046, Rd 108 & (15), Pr (17)
MP 1876, Ps 1051, Pr (17); DP 1056
EP 1878, Ps 1062, Pr (17); NP 1249

13. Sat. Saturday of the 19th Week in Ordinary Time
ALL 1067, Rd 113 & Pr 117; EP see below

OR: Sts. Pontian, Po & M, and Hippolytus, P & M (1312)
From Com of Mm 1694 or Pas 1748
OOR 1067, Rd 113 & 1313, Pr 1315
MP from Com, Ps 1072, Pr 1315; DP 1076; EP see below

OR: BVM on Saturday - 1656 & 1067
Rd 113 & 1656f, Pr 1667f; DP 1076
EP I (of Sunday) 1081, Ant & Pr 118; NP 1233

14. **Sun. TWENTIETH SUNDAY IN ORDINARY TIME**
ALL 1086, Rd, Te Deum, Ant & Pr 118
EP I (of Assumption) 1315; NP 1233

15. **Mon. ASSUMPTION OF THE BVM (Sol)**
ALL 1318, Te Deum; DP Ps 1255; NP 1236

16. Tue. Tuesday of the 20th Week in Ordinary Time
ALL 1129, Rd 128 & Pr 131; NP 1242

OR: St. Stephen of Hungary (1328)
From Com of HM 1818
OOR 1129, Rd 128 & 1328, Pr 1330
MP 1829, Ps 1134, Pr 1330; DP 1140
EP 1836, Ps 1145, Pr 1330; NP 1242

17. Wed. Wednesday of the 20th Week in Ordinary Time
ALL 1151, Rd 131 & Pr 135; NP 1244

18. Thu. Thursday of the 20th Week in Ordinary Time
ALL 1174, Rd 136 & Pr 140; NP 1247

19. Fri. Friday of the 20th Week in Ordinary Time
ALL 1194, Rd 140 & Pr 145; NP 1249

OR: St. John Eudes, P (1330)
From Com of Pas 1748 or Rel 1872
OOR 1194, Rd 140 & 1331, Pr 1332
MP from Com, Ps 1198, Pr 1332; DP 1204
EP from Com, Ps 1210, Pr 1332; NP 1249

20. Sat. St. Bernard, Ab & D (Mem) (1333)
From Com of D 1777 or Rel 1872
OOR 1214, Rd 145 & 1333, Pr 1335
MP from Com, Ps 1218, Ant & Pr 1335; DP 1223
EP I (of Sunday) 641, Ant & Pr 150; NP 1233

21. **Sun. TWENTY-FIRST SUNDAY IN ORDINARY TIME**
ALL 646, Rd, Te Deum, Ant & Pr 150; NP 1236

22. Mon. Queenship of Mary (Mem) (1338)
From Com of BVM 1628
OOR 666, Rd 155 & 1338, Pr 1341
MP 1640, Ps 670, Ant 1340 & Pr 1341; DP 675
EP 1648, Ps 681, Ant & Pr 1341; NP 1239

23. Tue. Tuesday of the 21st Week in Ordinary Time
ALL 686, Rd 160 & Pr 164; NP 1242

OR: St. Rose of Lima, V (1341)
From Com of V 1791 or Rel 1872
OOR 686, Rd 160 & 1342, Pr 1343
MP from Com, Ps 692, Pr 1343; DP 697
EP from Com, Ps 703, Pr 1343; NP 1242

24. Wed. ST. BARTHOLOMEW, AP (F) (1344)
From Com of Ap 1673 and Proper, Te Deum
DP 718, Rd, etc. 1682, Pr 1346; NP 1244

25. Thu. Thursday of the 21st Week in Ordinary Time
ALL 729, Rd 170 & Pr 174; NP 1247

OR: St. Louis (1347)
From Com of HM 1818
OOR 729, Rd 170 & 1347, Pr 1349
MP 1829, Ps 733, Pr 1349; DP 738
EP 1836, Ps 744, Pr 1349; NP 1247

OR: St. Joseph Calasanz, P (1349)
From Com of Tea 1885 or Pas 1748
OOR 729, Rd 170 & 1349, Pr 1351
MP from Com, Ps 733, Pr 1351; DP 738
EP from Com, Ps 744, Pr 1351; NP 1247

26. Fri. Friday of the 21st Week in Ordinary Time
ALL 750, Rd 175 & Pr 179; NP 1249

27. Sat. St. Monica (Mem) (1352)
From Com of HW 1849
OOR 771, Rd 180 & 1352, Pr 1354
MP 1857, Ps 775, Ant & Pr 1354; DP 780
EP I (of Sunday) 785, Ant & Pr 185; NP 1233

28. **Sun. TWENTY-SECOND SUNDAY IN ORDINARY TIME**
All 790, Rd, Te Deum, Ant & Pr 185; NP 1236

29. Mon. Beheading of St. John the Baptist, M (Mem) (1358)
From Com of M 1721
OOR 811, Rd 191 & 1358, Pr 1362
MP Hymn 1729, Ant 1360 & Ps 652, Rd, etc. 1361; DP 822
EP Hymn 1735, Ant 1362 & Ps 1736, Rd, etc. 1363; NP 1239

30. Tue. Tuesday of the 22nd Week in Ordinary Time
All 833, Rd 195 & Pr 199; NP 1242

31. Wed. Wednesday of the 22nd Week in Ordinary Time
All 855, Rd 199 & Pr 203; NP 1244

SEPTEMBER

1. Thu. Thursday of the 22nd Week in Ordinary Time
   ALL 880, Rd 204 & Pr 207; NP 1247

2. Fri. Friday of the 22nd Week in Ordinary Time
   All 901, Rd 208 & Pr 212; NP 1249

3. Sat. St. Gregory the Great, Po & D (Mem) (1365)
   From Com of Pas 1748 or D 1777
   OOR 922, Rd 213 & 1365, Pr 1367
   MP from Com, Ps 926, Ant & Pr 1367; DP 932
   EP I (of Sunday) 937, Ant & Pr 218; NP 1233

4. Sun. **TWENTY-THIRD SUNDAY IN ORDINARY TIME**
   All 942, Rd, Te Deum, Ant & Pr 218; NP 1236

5. Mon. Monday of the 23rd Week in Ordinary Time
   All 962, Rd 223 & Pr 227; NP 1239

6. Tue. Tuesday of the 23rd Week in Ordinary Time
   All 982, Rd 227 & Pr 232; NP 1242

7. Wed. Wednesday of the 23rd Week in Ordinary Time
   ALL 1003, Rd 232 & Pr 236; NP 1244

8. Thu. BIRTH OF MARY (F) (1368)
   From Com of BVM 1628 and Proper, Te Deum
   DP 1035, Rd, etc. 1373; NP 1247

9. Fri. St. Peter Claver, P (Mem) (2016)
   From Com of Pas 1748 or HM (Underpriv) 1880
   OOR 1046, Rd 243 & 2016, Pr 2019
   MP from Com, Ps 1051, Pr 2019; DP 1056
   EP from Com, Ps 1062, Pr 2019; NP 1249

10. Sat. Saturday of the 23rd Week in Ordinary Time
    ALL 1067, Rd 248 & Pr 251; EP see below

OR: BVM on Saturday - 1656 & 1067
    Rd 248 & 1656f, Pr 1667f; DP 1076
    EP I (of Sunday) 1081, Ant & Pr 252; NP 1233

11. Sun. **TWENTY-FOURTH SUNDAY IN ORDINARY TIME**
    ALL 1086, Rd, Te Deum, Ant & Pr 252; NP 1236

12. Mon. Monday of the 24th Week in Ordinary Time
    ALL 1107, Rd 256 & Pr 260; NP 1239

OR: Most Holy Name of Mary *(New)*
From Com of BVM 1628
OOR 1107, Rd 256 & 1635f, Pr 1645f
MP 1640, Ps 1112, Pr 1645f; DP 1118
EP 1648, Ps 1124, Pr 1645f; NP 1239

13. Tue. St. John Chrysostom, B & D (Mem) (1376)
From Com of Pas 1748 or D 1777
OOR 1129, Rd 260 & 1377, Pr 1379
MP from Com, Ps 1134, Pr 1379; DP 1140
EP from Com, Ps 1145; Pr 1379; NP 1242

14. Wed. TRIUMPH OF THE CROSS (F)
ALL 1384, Te Deum; DP Ps 1162; EP 1396; NP 1244

15. Thu. Our Lady of Sorrows (Mem) (1401)
From Com of BVM 1628
OOR 1174, Rd 269 & 1401, Pr 1404
MP Hymn 1640, Ant 1403 & Ps 652, Rd, etc. 1403; DP 1183
EP 1648, Ant 1404 & Ps 1649, Rd, etc. 1404; NP 1247

16. Fri. Sts. Cornelius, Po & M and Cyprian, B & M (Mem) (1406)
From Com of Mm 1694 or Pas 1748
OOR 1194, Rd 273 & 1406, Pr 1410
MP from Com, Ps 1198, Ant & Pr 1410; DP 1204
EP from Com, Ps 1210, Ant 1411, Pr 1410; NP 1249

17. Sat. Saturday of the 24th Week in Ordinary Time
ALL 1214, Rd 278 & Pr 282; EP see below

OR: St. Robert Bellarmine, B & D (1411)
From Com of Pas 1748 or D 1777
OOR 1214, Rd 278 & 1411, Pr 1413
MP from Com, Ps 1218, Pr 1413; DP 1223; EP see below

OR: BVM on Saturday - 1656 & 1214
Rd 278 & 1656f, Pr 1667f; DP 1223
EP I (of Sunday) 641, Ant & Pr 283; NP 1233

18. **Sun. TWENTY-FIFTH SUNDAY IN ORDINARY TIME**
ALL 646, Rd, Te Deum, Ant & Pr 283; NP 1236

19. Mon. Monday of the 25th Week in Ordinary Time
ALL 666, Rd 287 & Pr 291; NP 1239

OR: St. Januarius, B & M (1413)
       From Com of M 1721 or Pas 1748
       OOR 666, Rd 287 & 1414, Pr 1416
       MP from Com, Ps 670, Pr 1416; DP 675
       EP from Com, Ps 681, Pr 1416; NP 1239

20.   Tue. Sts. Andrew Kim Taegŏn, P & M, Paul Chŏng Hasang, and Comps,
       Mm (Mem) **(New)** (17)
       From Com of Mm 1694
       OOR 686, Rd 292 & (18) or 1700, Pr (21) or 1706
       MP from Com, Ps 692, Pr (21) or 1706; DP 697
       EP from Com, Ps 703, Pr (21) or 1706; NP 1242

21.   Wed. ST. MATTHEW, AP & EVANGELIST (F) (1416)
       From Com of Ap 1673 and Proper, Te Deum
       DP 718, Rd, etc. 1682, Pr 1420; NP 1244

22.   Thu. Thursday of the 25th Week in Ordinary Time
       ALL 729, Rd 300 & Pr 304; NP 1247

23.   Fri. St. Pius of Pietrelcina, P (Mem) *(New)*
       From Com of Pas 1748
       OOR 750, Rd 304 & 1759, Pr 1767
       MP from Com, Ps 754, Pr 1767; DP 760
       EP from Com, Ps 766, 1767; NP 1249

24.   Sat. Saturday of the 25th Week in Ordinary Time
       ALL 771, Rd 309 & Pr 312; EP see below

OR: BVM on Saturday - 1656 & 771
       Rd 309 & 1656f, Pr 1667f; DP 780
       EP I (of Sunday) 785, Ant & Pr 313; NP 1233

25.   **Sun. TWENTY-SIXTH SUNDAY IN ORDINARY TIME**
       ALL 790, Rd, Te Deum, Ant & Pr 313; NP 1236

26.   Mon. Monday of the 26th Week in Ordinary Time
       ALL 811, Rd 317 & Pr 320; NP 1239

OR: Sts. Cosmas and Damian, Mm (1421)
       From Com of Mm 1694
       OOR 811, Rd 317 & 1421, Pr 1423
       MP 1702, Ps 817, Pr 1423; DP 822
       EP 1708, Ps 828, Pr 1423; NP 1239

27.   Tue. St. Vincent de Paul, P (Mem) (1423)
       From Com of Pas 1748 or HM (Underpriv) 1880
       OOR 833, Rd 321 & 1424, Pr 1426

MP from Com, Ps 839, Ant & Pr 1426; DP 845
EP from Com, Ps 850, Ant & Pr 1426; NP 1242

28. Wed. Wednesday of the 26th Week in Ordinary Time
ALL 855, Rd 325 & Pr 328; NP 1244

OR: St. Wenceslaus, M (1426)
From Com of M 1721
OOR 855, Rd 325 & 1427, Pr 1428
MP 1729, Ps 861, Pr 1428; DP 867
EP 1735, Ps 874, Pr 1428; NP 1244

OR: St. Lawrence Ruiz and Comps, Mm **(New)** (21)
From Com of Mm 1694
OOR 855, Rd 325 & Proper (22) or 1700, Pr proper (24) or 1706
MP 1702, Ps 861, Pr proper (24) or 1706; DP 867
EP 1708, Ps 874, Pr proper (24) or 1713; NP 1244

29. Thu. STS. MICHAEL, GABRIEL AND RAPHAEL, ARCHANGELS (F)
ALL 1429, Te Deum, DP Ps 890; NP 1247

30. Fri. St. Jerome, P & D (Mem) (1447)
From Com of D 1777
OOR 901, Rd 332 & 1447, Pr 1449
MP 1782, Ps 905, Ant 1783, Pr 1449; DP 910
EP 1784, Ps 916, Ant 1785, Pr 1449; NP 1249

OCTOBER

1. Sat. St. Theresa of the Child Jesus, V & D (Mem) (1450)
From Com of V 1791 or D 1777
OOR 923, Rd 336 & 1450, Pr 1452
MP from Com, Ps 926, Ant & Pr 1452; DP 932
EP I (of Sunday) 937, Ant & Pr 340; NP 1233

2. **Sun. TWENTY-SEVENTH SUNDAY IN ORDINARY TIME**
ALL 942, Rd, Te Deum, Ant & Pr 340; NP 1236

3. Mon. Monday of the 27th Week in Ordinary Time
ALL 962, Rd 345 & Pr 348; NP 1239

4. Tue. St. Francis of Assisi (Mem) (1465)
From Com of Rel 1872
OOR 982, Rd 349 & 1465, Pr 1467
MP 1876, Ps 988, Ant & Pr 1467; DP 993
EP 1878, Ps 998, Ant 1468, Pr 1467; NP 1242

5. Wed. Wednesday of the 27th Week in Ordinary Time
ALL 1003, Rd 353 & Pr 357; NP 1244

OR: St. Faustina Kowalska, V *(New)*
From Com of V 1791 or Rel 1872
OOR 1003, Rd 353 & 1796, Pr 1803 or 1877
MP from Com, Ps 1009, Pr 1803 or 1877; DP 1014
EP from Com, Ps 1020, Pr 1811 or 1877; NP 1244

OR: Bl. Francis Xavier Seelos, P *(New)*
From Com of Pas 1748
OOR 1003, Rd 353 & 1752, Pr 1767
MP 1763, Ps 1009, Pr 1767; DP 1014
EP 1769, Ps 1020, Pr 1775; NP 1244

6. Thu. Thursday of the 27th Week in Ordinary Time
ALL 1025, Rd 357 & Pr 361; NP 1247

OR: St. Bruno, P (1468)
From Com of Pas 1748 or Rel 1872
OOR 1025, Rd 357 & 1468, Pr 1470
MP from Com, Ps 1030, Pr 1470; DP 1035
EP from Com, Ps 1041, Pr 1470; NP 1247

OR: Bl. Marie Rose Durocher, V **(New)** (24)
From Com of V 1791
OOR 1025, Rd 357 & 1796, Pr proper (25) or 1803
MP 1800, Ps 1030, Pr proper (25) or 1803; DP 1035
EP 1805, Ps 1041, Pr proper (25) or 1811; NP 1247

7. Fri. Our Lady of the Rosary (Mem) (1470)
From Com of BVM 1628
OOR 1046, Rd 362 & 1470, Pr 1473
MP 1472, Ps 652, Pr 1473; DP 1056
EP 1474, Ps 1649, Pr 1473; NP 1249

8. Sat. Saturday of the 27th Week in Ordinary Time
ALL 1067, Rd 366 & Pr 369; EP see below

OR: BVM on Saturday - 1656 & 1067
Rd 366 & 1656f, Pr 1667f; DP 1076
EP I (of Sunday) 1081, Ant & Pr 370; NP 1233

9. Sun. **TWENTY-EIGHTH SUNDAY IN ORDINARY TIME**
ALL 1086, Rd, Te Deum, Ant & Pr 370; NP 1236

10. Mon. Monday of the 28th Week in Ordinary Time
ALL 1107, Rd 376 & Pr 379; NP 1239

11. Tue. Tuesday of the 28th Week in Ordinary Time
    ALL 1129, Rd 380 & Pr 384; NP 1242

OR: St. John XXIII, Po *(New)*
    From Com of Pas 1748
    OOR 1129, Rd 380 & 1754, Pr 1766
    MP 1763, Ps 1134, Pr 1766, DP 1140
    EP 1769, Ps 1145, Pr 1774; NP 1242

12. Wed. Wednesday of the 28th Week in Ordinary Time
    ALL 1151, Rd 384 & Pr 388; NP 1244

13. Thu. Thursday of the 28th Week in Ordinary Time
    ALL 1174, Rd 389 & Pr 393; NP 1247

14. Fri. Friday of the 28th Week in Ordinary Time
    ALL 1194, Rd 394 & Pr 399; NP 1249

OR: St. Callistus I, Po & M (1480)
    From Com of M 1721 or Pas 1748
    OOR 1194, Rd 394 & 1480, Pr 1482
    MP from Com, Ps 1198, Pr 1482; DP 1204
    EP from Com, Ps 1210, Pr 1482; NP 1249

15. Sat. St. Teresa of Avila, V & D (Mem) (1482)
    From Com of V 1791 or D 1777
    OOR 1214, Rd 399 & 1483, Pr 1484
    MP from Com, Ps 1218, Pr 1484; DP 1223
    EP I (of Sunday) 641, Ant & Pr 405; NP 1233

16. Sun. **TWENTY-NINTH SUNDAY IN ORDINARY TIME**
    ALL 646, Rd, Te Deum, Ant & Pr 405; NP 1236

17. Mon. St. Ignatius of Antioch, B & M (Mem) (1490)
    From Com of M 1721 or Pas 1748
    OOR 666, Rd 410 & 1490, Pr 1492
    MP from Com, Ps 670, Ant & Pr 1492; DP 675
    EP from Com, Ps 681, Ant 1493, Pr 1492; NP 1239

18. Tue. ST. LUKE, EVANGELIST (F) (1493)
    From Com of Ap 1673 and Proper, Te Deum
    DP 697, Rd, etc. 1499, Te Deum; NP 1242

19. Wed. Sts. Isaac Jogues and John de Brébeuf, Pp & Mm, and Comps,
    Mm (Mem) (2019)
    From Com of Mm 1694 or Pas 1748
    OOR 708, Rd 419 & 2020, Pr 2021

MP from Com, Ps 713, Pr 2021; DP 718
EP from Com, Ps 723, Pr 2021; NP 1244

20. Thu. Thursday of the 29th Week in Ordinary Time
ALL 729, Rd 423 & Pr 426; NP 1247

OR: St. Paul of the Cross, P (1505) **[transferred from 10/19]**
From Com of Pas 1748 or Rel 1872
OOR 729, Rd 423 & 1505, Pr 1507
MP from Com, Ps 733, Pr 1507; DP 738
EP from Com, Ps 744, Pr 1507; NP 1247

21. Fri. Friday of the 29th Week in Ordinary Time
ALL 750, Rd 427 & Pr 431; NP 1249

22. Sat. Saturday of the 29th Week in Ordinary Time
ALL 771, Rd 431 & Pr 436; EP see below

OR: St. John Paul II, Po *(New)*
From Com of Pas 1748
OOR 771, Rd 431 & 1754, Pr 1766
MP 1763, Ps 775, Pr 1766; DP 780; EP see below

OR: BVM on Saturday - 1656 & 771
Rd 431 & 1656f, Pr 1667f; DP 780
EP I (of Sunday) 785, Ant & Pr 437; NP 1233

23. **Sun. THIRTIETH SUNDAY IN ORDINARY TIME**
ALL 790, Rd, Te Deum, Ant & Pr 437; NP 1236

24. Mon. Monday of the 30th Week in Ordinary Time
ALL 811, Rd 441 & Pr 445; NP 1239

OR: St. Anthony Claret, B (1510)
From Com of Pas 1748
OOR 811, Rd 441 & 1510, Pr 1511
MP 1763, Ps 817, Pr 1511; DP 822
EP 1769, Ps 828, Pr 1511; NP 1239

25. Tue. Tuesday of the 30th Week in Ordinary Time
ALL 833, Rd 446 & Pr 449; NP 1242

26. Wed. Wednesday of the 30th Week in Ordinary Time
ALL 855, Rd 450 & Pr 454; NP 1244

27. Thu. Thursday of the 30th Week in Ordinary Time
ALL 880, Rd 454 & Pr 458; NP 1247

28. Fri. STS. SIMON AND JUDE, AP (F) (1512)
From Com of Ap 1673 and Proper, Te Deum
DP 910, Rd, etc. 1682, Pr 1514; NP 1249

29. Sat. Saturday of the 30th Week in Ordinary Time
ALL 922, Rd 463 & Pr 467; EP see below

OR: BVM on Saturday - 1656 & 922
Rd 463 & 1656f, Pr 1667f; DP 932
EP I (of Sunday) 937, Ant & Pr 468; NP 1233

30. Sun. **THIRTY-FIRST SUNDAY IN ORDINARY TIME**
ALL 942, Rd, Te Deum, Ant & Pr 468; NP 1236

31. Mon. Monday of the 31st Week in Ordinary Time
ALL 962, Rd 473 & Pr 477
EP I (of All Saints) 1515; NP 1233

NOVEMBER

1. Tue. **ALL SAINTS (Sol)**
ALL 1520, Te Deum; DP Ps 1255; NP 1236

2. Wed. ALL SOULS (1537)
From Office for the Dead 1891 and Proper; NP 1236

3. Thu. Thursday of the 31st Week in Ordinary Time
ALL 1025, Rd 486 & Pr 490; NP 1247

OR: St. Martin de Porres, Rel (1540)
From Com of Rel 1872
OOR 1025, Rd 486 & 1541, Pr 1543
MP 1876, Ps 1030, Ant & Pr 1543; DP 1035
EP 1878, Ps 1041, Ant & Pr 1543; NP 1247

4. Fri. St. Charles Borromeo, B (Mem) (1543)
From Com of Pas 1748
OOR 1046, Rd 491 & 1544, Pr 1546
MP 1763, Ps 1051, Pr 1546; DP 1056
EP 1769, Ps 1062, Pr 1546; NP 1249

5. Sat. Saturday of the 31st Week in Ordinary Time
ALL 1067, Rd 495 & Pr 499; EP see below

OR: BVM on Saturday - 1656 & 1067
Rd 495 & 1656f, 1667f; DP 1076
EP I (of Sunday) 1081, Ant & Pr 500; NP 1233

6. **Sun. THIRTY-SECOND SUNDAY IN ORDINARY TIME**
ALL 1086, Rd, Te Deum, Ant & Pr 500; NP 1236

7. Mon. Monday of the 32nd Week in Ordinary Time
ALL 1107, Rd 505 & Pr 510; NP 1239

8. Tue. Tuesday of the 32nd Week in Ordinary Time
ALL 1129, Rd 510 & Pr 514; NP 1242

9. Wed. DEDICATION OF SAINT JOHN LATERAN (F) (1546)
From Com of Ded 1600 and Proper, Te Deum
DP 1161, Rd, etc. 1612, Pr 1611; EP 1614; NP 1244

10. Thu. St. Leo the Great, Po & D (Mem) (1548)
From Com of Pas 1748 or D 1777
OOR 1174, Rd 518 & 1549, Pr 1551
MP from Com, Ps 1178, Ant & Pr 1551; DP 1183
EP from Com, Ps 1189, Ant & Pr 1551; NP 1247

11. Fri. St. Martin of Tours, B (Mem) (1551)
From Com of Pas 1748
OOR 1195, Rd 523 & 1552, Pr 1555
MP Hymn 1763, Ant 1554, Ps 652, Rd, etc. 1554; DP 1204
EP Hymn 1769, Ant 1555, Ps 1770, Rd, etc.1555; NP 1249

12. Sat. St. Josaphat, B & M (Mem) (1556)
From Com of M 1721 or Pas 1748
OOR 1214, Rd 527 & 1557, Pr 1558
MP from Com, Ps 1218, Pr 1558; DP 1223
EP I (of Sunday) 641, Ant & Pr 532; NP 1233

13. **Sun. THIRTY-THIRD SUNDAY IN ORDINARY TIME**
ALL 646, Rd, Te Deum, Ant & Pr 532; NP 1236

14. Mon. Monday of the 33rd Week in Ordinary Time
ALL 666, Rd 538 & Pr 542; NP 1239

15. Tue. Tuesday of the 33rd Week in Ordinary Time
ALL 686, Rd 542 & Pr 547; NP 1242

OR: St. Albert the Great, B & D (1559)
From Com of Pas 1748 or D 1777
OOR 686, Rd 542 & 1559, Pr 1561
MP from Com, Ps 692, Pr 1561; DP 697
EP from Com, Ps 703, Pr 1561; NP 1242

16. Wed. Wednesday of the 33rd Week in Ordinary Time
ALL 708, Rd 548 & Pr 552; NP 1244

OR: St. Margaret of Scotland (1561)
From Com of HW (Underpriv) 1880
OOR 708, Rd 548 & 1562, Pr 1563
MP 1857, Ps 713, Ant 1883, Pr 1563; DP 718
EP 1863, Ps 723, Ant 1884, Pr 1563; NP 1244

OR: St. Gertrude, V (1564)
From Com of V 1791 or Rel 1872
OOR 709, Rd 548 & 1564, Pr 1566
MP from Com, Ps 713, Pr 1566; DP 718
EP from Com, Ps 723, Pr 1566; NP 1244

17. Thu. St. Elizabeth of Hungary (Mem) (1567)
From Com of HW (Underpriv) 1880
OOR 729, Rd 552 & 1567, Pr 1569
MP 1857, Ps 733, Ant 1883, Pr 1569; DP 738
EP 1863, Ps 744, Ant 1884, Pr 1569; NP 1247

18. Fri. Friday of the 33rd Week in Ordinary Time
ALL 750, Rd 557 & Pr 560; NP 1249

OR: Ded. of the Churches of Sts. Peter and Paul, Ap (1569)
From Com of Ap 1673
OOR 750, Rd 557 & 1570, Pr 1571
MP 1680, Ps 754, Ant & Pr 1571; DP 760
EP 1683, Ps 766, Ant 1572 & Pr 1571; NP 1249

OR: St. Rose Philippine Duchesne, V **(New)** (26)
From Com of V 1791
OOR 750, Rd 557 & 1796, Pr proper (26) or 1803
MP 1800, Ps 754, Pr proper (26) or 1803; DP 760
EP 1805, Ps 766, Pr proper (26) or 1811; NP 1249

19. Sat. Saturday of the 33rd Week in Ordinary Time
ALL 771, Rd 561 & Pr 565; EP see below

OR: BVM on Saturday - 1656 & 771
Rd 561 & 1656f, Pr 1667f; DP 780
EP I (of Christ the King) 566; NP 1233

20. **Sun. CHRIST THE KING (Sol)**
ALL 570, Te Deum; DP 657; NP 1236

21. Mon. Presentation of Mary (Mem) (1572)
From Com of BVM 1628
OOR 811, Rd 587 & 1572, Pr 1575

MP 1640, Ps 817, Ant & Pr 1575; DP 822
EP 1648, Ps 828, Ant & Pr 1575; NP 1239

22. Tue. St. Cecilia, V & M (Mem) (1575)
From Com of M 1721 or V 1791
OOR 833, Rd 590 & 1576, Pr 1578
MP from Com, Ps 839, Ant & Pr 1578; DP 845
EP from Com, Ps 850, Ant & Pr 1578; NP 1242

23. Wed. Wednesday of the 34th Week in Ordinary Time
ALL 855, Rd 594 & Pr 597; NP 1244

OR: St. Clement I, Po & M (1578)
From Com of M 1721 or Pas 1748
OOR 855, Rd 594 & 1579, Pr 1580
MP from Com, Ps 861, Pr 1580; DP 867
EP from Com, Ps 874, Pr 1580; NP 1244

OR: St. Columban, Ab (1581)
From Com of Pas 1748 or Rel 1872
OOR 855, Rd 594 & 1581, Pr 1583
MP from Com, Ps 861, Pr 1583; DP 867
EP from Com, Ps 874, Pr 1583; NP 1244

OR: Bl. Miguel Agustín Pro, P & M **(New)** (27)
From Com of M 1721 or Pas 1748
OOR 855, Rd 594 & 1726 or 1752, Pr proper (28) or 1733 or 1767
MP from Com, Ps 861, Pr as above; DP 867
EP from Com, Ps 874, Pr as above; NP 1244

24. Thu. St. Andrew Dung-Lac, P, and Comps, Mm (Mem) **(New)** (28)
From Com of Mm 1694
OOR 880, Rd 597 & (29), Pr proper (31) or 1706
MP 1702, Ps 884, Pr proper (31) or 1706; DP 890
EP 1708, Ps 896; Pr proper (31) or 1713; NP 1247

25. Fri. Friday of the 34th Week in Ordinary Time
ALL 901, Rd 601 & Pr 605; NP 1249

OR: St. Catherine of Alexandria, V & M *(New)*
From Com of M 1721 or V 1791
OOR 901, Rd 601 & 1726 or 1796f, Pr 1733
MP from Com, Ps 905, Pr 1733; DP 910
EP from Com, Ps 916, Pr 1741; NP 1249

26. Sat. Saturday of the 34th Week in Ordinary Time
ALL 922, Rd 606 & Pr 610; EP see next volume (I)

OR: BVM on Saturday - 1656 & 922
Rd 606 & 1656f, Pr 1667f; DP 932; EP see next volume (I)

BEGIN VOLUME I

EP I (of Sunday) 137, Hymn 126 or 677, Ps 678; NP 1169

27. **Sun. FIRST SUNDAY OF ADVENT**
OOR 139, Hymn 121 or 682, Ps 683, Te Deum, Pr 146
MP 144, Hymn 122 or 687, Ps 687; DP 691, Ant, etc. 146
EP II 148, Hymn 126 or 694, Ps 695; NP 1172

28. Mon. Monday of the 1st Week of Advent
ALL 699, Ant, Rd, etc. 150; NP 1175

29. Tue. Tuesday of the 1st Week of Advent
ALL 714, Ant, Rd, etc. 158; NP 1178

30. Wed. ST. ANDREW, AP (F) (1201)
From Com of Ap 1354 and Proper, Te Deum
DP 741, Ant 167, Rd, etc. 1363, Pr 1207; NP 1180

DECEMBER

1. Thu. Thursday of the 1st Week of Advent
ALL 749, Ant, Rd, etc. 175; NP 1183

2. Fri. Friday of the 1st Week of Advent
ALL 765, Ant, Rd, etc. 183; NP 1185

3. Sat. St. Francis Xavier, P (Mem) (1210)
From Com of Pas 1428
OOR 1428, Ps 782, Rd 190 & 1210, Pr 1212
MP 1443, Ps 787, Pr 1212; DP 789, Ant, etc. 195
EP I (of Sunday) 197, Hymn 126 or 793, Ps 794; NP 1169

4. **Sun. SECOND SUNDAY OF ADVENT**
OOR 199, Hymn 121 or 798, Ps 798, Te Deum, Pr 205
MP 203, Hymn 122 or 802, Ps 804; DP 808, Ant, etc. 206
EP II 207, Hymn 126 or 811, Ps 811; NP 1172

5. Mon. Monday of the 2nd Week of Advent
ALL 816, Ant, Rd, etc. 209; NP 1175

6. Tue. Tuesday of the 2nd Week of Advent
ALL 833, Ant, Rd, etc. 218; NP 1178

OR: St. Nicholas, B (1215)
From Com of Pas 1428
OOR 1428, Ps 834, Rd 218 & 1215, Pr 1217
MP 1443, Ps 839, Pr 1217; DP 844, Ant, etc. 222
EP 1449, Ps 847, Pr 1217; NP 1178

7. Wed. St. Ambrose, B & D (Mem) (1217)
From Com of D 1458
OOR 1458, Ps 852, Rd 225 & 1218, Pr 1220
MP 1464, Ps 857, Pr 1220; DP 862, Ant, etc. 230
EP I (of Immaculate Conception) 1221; NP 1169

8. **Thu. IMMACULATE CONCEPTION (Sol)**
ALL 1224, Te Deum; DP Ps 1191; NP 1172

9. Fri. Friday of the 2nd Week of Advent
ALL 890, Ant, Rd, etc. 242; NP 1185

OR: St. Juan Diego **(New)** (32)
From Com of HM 1500
OOR 1500, Ps 891, Rd 242 & 1508, Pr proper (33) or 1516
MP 1512, Ps 894, Pr proper (33) or 1516; DP 898, Ant, Rd, etc. 247
EP 1519, Ps 902, Pr proper (33) or 1524; NP 1185

10. Sat. Saturday of the 2nd Week of Advent
ALL 906, Ant, Rd, etc. 250; EP see below

OR: Our Lady of Loreto *(New)*
From Com of BVM 1326
OOR 1326, Ps 907, Rd 250 & 1332f, Pr p. 47 of this Guide
MP 1337, Ps 912, Pr p. 47 of this Guide; DP 916, Ant, Rd, etc. 1342
EP I (of Sunday) 256, Hymn 126 or 920, Ps 921; NP 1169

11. **Sun. THIRD SUNDAY OF ADVENT**
OOR Ant at Invit 258, Hymn 121, Ps 925, Rd & Responsories 259,
Te Deum, Pr 264
MP 263, Hymn 122 or 928, Ps 929, Rd, Ant & Intercessions 263
DP Hymn 658, Ps 934, Ant, etc. 265
EP II 266, Hymn 126 or 937, Ps 937, Rd, Ant & Intercessions 266,
Pr 268
NP 1172

12. Mon. OUR LADY OF GUADALUPE (F) **(New)** (33)
From Com of BVM 1326 and Proper; Invit (33)
OOR (34), Ps 1328, Rd (35), Te Deum, Pr (42)

MP (42), Ps 688, Pr (45); DP 949, Ant, etc. 1342
EP (46), Ps 1345, Pr (48); NP 1175

13. Tue. St. Lucy, V & M (Mem) (1242)
From Com of M 1401 or V 1473
OOR from Com, Ps 958, Rd 277 & 1242, Pr 1245
MP from Com, Ps 963, Ant & Pr 1245; DP 967, Ant, etc. 282
EP from Com, Ps 971, Ant & Pr 1245; NP 1178

14. Wed. St. John of the Cross, P & D (Mem) (1245)
From Com of D 1458
OOR 1458, Ps 976, Rd 285 & 1246, Pr 1247
MP 1464, Ps 981, Pr 1247; DP 986, Ant, etc. 290
EP 1466, Ps 989, Pr 1247; NP 1180

15. Thu. Thursday of the 3rd Week of Advent
ALL 994, Ant, Rd, etc. 293; NP 1183

16. Fri. Friday of the 3rd Week of Advent
ALL 1012, Ant, Rd, etc. 300; NP 1185

17. Sat. Saturday of the 3rd Week of Advent
ALL 1030, Ant at Invit 647, Ant, Rd, etc. 318, Pr 323
EP I (of Sunday) 309, Hymn 133 or 1042, Ps 1043, Ant at Mag 325
NP 1169

18. **Sun. FOURTH SUNDAY OF ADVENT**
OOR 311 & 326, Hymn 132 or 1047, Ps 1048, Te Deum, Pr 313
MP 312, Hymn 132 or 1051, Ps 1053; DP 1057, Ant, etc. 314
EP II 315, Hymn 133 or 1060, Ps 1060, Ant at Mag 333, Intercessions &
Pr 316; NP 1172

19. Mon. Monday of the 4th Week of Advent
ALL 1064, Ant, Rd, etc. 334, Pr 340; NP 1175

20. Tue. Tuesday of the 4th Week of Advent
ALL 1082, Ant, Rd, etc. 343, Pr 347; NP 1178

21. Wed. Wednesday of the 4th Week of Advent
OOR 1099, Rd 351, Pr 356 (May add Rd of St. Peter Canisius, P & D,
with his Pr 1249-1250)
MP 1103, Rd, etc. 355 (May add Ant & Pr of St. Peter 1249)
DP 1109, Ant, Rd, etc. 356
EP 1112, Rd, etc. 358 (May add Ant 1250 & Pr of St. Peter 1249)
NP 1180

22. Thu. Thursday of the 4th Week of Advent
ALL 1118, Ant, Rd, etc. 359, Pr 365; NP 1183

23. Fri. Friday of the 4th Week of Advent
    OOR 1135, Rd 368, Pr 373 (May add Rd of St. John of Kanty, P, with his
        Pr 1250-1252)
    MP 1140, Rd, etc. 372 (May add Ant & Pr of St. John of Kanty 1252)
    DP 1145, Ant, Rd, etc. 374
    EP 1148, Rd, etc. 375 (May add Ant & Pr of St. John of Kanty 1252)
    NP 1185

24. Sat. Saturday of the 4th Week of Advent
    ALL 1152, Ant at Invit 376, Rd, etc. 377
    MP 381, Ps 1157; DP 383, Ps 1160; EP I of Christmas ALL 394
    NP 1169 (if not present at OOR & Midnight Mass)

25. **Sun. CHRISTMAS (Sol)**
    OOR 399, Te Deum and Prayer 406 only if Mass does not follow; if Mass
        follows, say the Gloria (without introductory rite[s]) followed by
        Opening Prayer [Collect] of Mass.
    MP (Not after Midnight Mass, but in Morning) ALL 407
    DP 409; EP 414; NP 1169 or 1172

26. Mon. ST. STEPHEN, FIRST M (F) (1253)
    From Com of M 1401 and Proper; Te Deum
    DP 707, Ant, Rd, etc. 1260, Pr 1259
    EP (as Christmas) 414, Rd, etc. 436; NP 1169 or 1172

27. Tue. ST. JOHN, AP & EVANGELIST (F) (1261)
    From Com of Ap 1354 and Proper, Te Deum
    DP 725, Ant, Rd, etc. 1270, Pr 1270
    EP (as Christmas) 414, Rd, etc. 438; NP 1169 or 1172

28. Wed. HOLY INNOCENTS, MM (F) (1272)
    From Com of Mm 1375 and Proper, Te Deum
    DP 741, Ant, Rd, etc. 1277, Pr 1277
    EP 414, Rd, etc. 440; NP 1169 or 1172

29. Thu. FIFTH DAY IN THE OCTAVE OF CHRISTMAS
    OOR 442, Te Deum, Pr 450 (May add Rd of St. Thomas Becket, B & M,
        with his Pr 1279-1281)
    MP 407, Rd, etc. 448 (May add Ant & Pr of St. Thomas 1281)
    DP 757, Ant, Rd, etc. 450
    EP 414, Rd, etc. 451 (May add Ant 1282 & Pr of St. Thomas 1281)
    NP 1169 or 1172

30. Fri. HOLY FAMILY (F) (424)
    From Com of BVM 1326 & Proper, Te Deum

DP 773, Hymn 385, Ant, Rd, etc. 431
EP II 432; NP 1169 or 1172

31. Sat. SEVENTH DAY IN THE OCTAVE OF CHRISTMAS
    OOR 466, Te Deum, Pr 474 (May add Rd of St. Sylvester I, Po with his
        Pr 1282-1284)
    MP 407, Rd, etc. 473 (May add Ant & Pr of St. Sylvester 1284)
    DP 789, Ant, Rd, etc. 474
    EP I (of Mary) 476; NP 1169

Prayers

(For use on June 6, The Blessed Virgin Mary, Mother of the Church [Memorial])

O God, Father of mercies,
whose Only Begotten Son, as he hung upon the Cross,
chose the Blessed Virgin Mary, his Mother,
to be our Mother also,
grant, we pray, that with her loving help
your Church may be more fruitful day by day
and, exulting in the holiness of her children,
may draw to her embrace all the families of the peoples.
Through our Lord Jesus Christ, your Son,
who lives and reigns with you in the unity of the Holy Spirit,
God, for ever and ever.

(For use on December 10, Our Lady of Loreto [Optional Memorial])

O God, who, fulfilling the promise made to our Fathers,
chose the Blessed Virgin Mary
to become the Mother of the Savior,
grant that we may follow her example,
for her humility was pleasing to you
and her obedience profitable to us.
Through our Lord Jesus Christ, your Son,
who lives and reigns with you in the unity of the Holy Spirit,
God, for ever and ever.

The
LITURGY OF THE HOURS
is truly the prayer of the Church
for all the people of God –
bishops, priests, deacons,
religious and the
laity.

ISBN 978-1-953152-39-8

90000

This Guide is No. 709/G
ISBN 978-1-953152-39-8